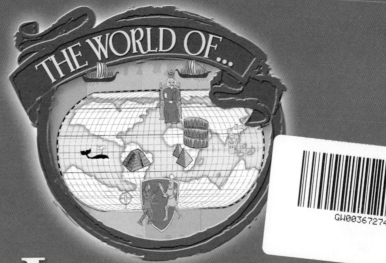

THE WORLD OF...

History
Revision

Lynn Huggins-Cooper

Good day. I'm Sir Ralph Witherbottom. I'm an accomplished inventor, a dashing discoverer and an enthusiastic entrepreneur.

Hi! I'm Isabella Witherbottom – my friends call me Izzy. I'm Sir Ralph's daughter and I like to keep him on his toes!

And they both keep me on my toes! How do you do? I'm Max, the butler, at your service.

Woof! I'm Spotless – aptly named, as you can see. I'm the family's loyal dog.

Contents

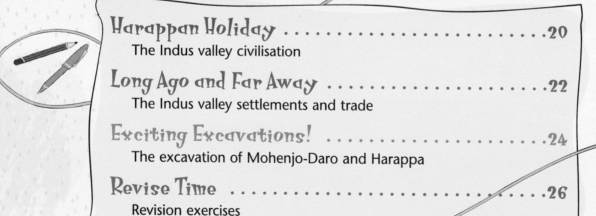

A Greek Odyssey

Max, the butler, Sir Ralph and Isabella Witherbottom are on holiday in Greece. They are walking around the **ruins** of some ancient Greek baths. Sir Ralph wants to visit as many ancient Greek sites as possible, but Isabella is not so sure!

"Dad, can't we just go back to the beach? I'm hot! When you said we were going to 'the baths', I thought you meant swimming baths – not this old ruin!" moaned Isabella, looking down the hill at the sparkling blue sea.

"Soon, Izzy. This place is quite wonderful, though. The sense of history… It's amazing to think that ancient Greece had a sophisticated **culture** so long ago! The first Olympic Games were held in 776 **BC** – the BC means 'Before Christ'. That's nearly 3000 years ago! You know my favourite book – the '**Odyssey**', by Homer?" said Sir Ralph.

"Of course, dad! I loved those stories when I was little; and the stories of the '**Iliad**', too," she replied.

Yes, you're loud enough to be a siren!

"They were written in 750 BC. That's incredible, isn't it? In Britain at the time, we were still in the **Bronze Age**!" said Sir Ralph. "Just think of the great minds who may have bathed right here, whilst they pondered great ideas."

"Wow. That is an amazing thought. I can see why you wanted to come here now. I'd still like to go for a swim though, dad. Come on – last one in the sea's a sea monster!" called Isabella, as she ran down the hill towards the sea.

Missing words

Write about the ancient Greeks by filling in the gaps.

1 Ancient Greece had a _Sophisticated_ culture.

2 The first Olympic Games were held in _776 Bc_.

3 The _Odyssey_ and the _Iliad_ were written by Homer.

4 When ancient Greek civilisation was at its peak, Britain was still in the
Bronze age..

5 _Baths_ were used by many people,

including all the great thinkers of the ancient Greek age.

6 BC means _Before christ_.

Top Tips

The Odyssey is full of adventures! Read 'The Wanderings
of Odysseus' by Rosemary Sutcliffe and 'Homer's
Odyssey', a dramatisation by David Calcutt.

Did you know?

The ancient Greeks took a variety of baths. These included hot water tubs
and hot-air baths, called laconica. Hot-air baths were often heated by the hot
rock method, which meant heating the rocks before taking them into the hot
room. The people of Laconia, the region of Greece with Sparta as a capital,
invented the idea.

Spiteful Spartans!

Sir Ralph Witherbottom was telling Max, the butler, and Isabella a little more about ancient Greece.

"Have you ever heard the saying 'That's a bit Spartan'? It means things are without comfort. Spartan boys went away from their parents at age seven to live in the soldiers' **barracks**. They were beaten and whipped by older children. They weren't allowed to cry out in pain. They weren't fed very much and were encouraged to steal food instead. If they were caught, they were beaten. This was to teach the boys to be cunning, fierce and capable."

"That's terrible, dad! What about Athens – was it the same there?" asked Isabella.

"Not at all, Izzy! Athenians were cultured people. Athenian children were taught at home by their mother until they were seven. Then they were sent to a day school, just like you. They learned drama, reading, writing, mathematics, public speaking and music.

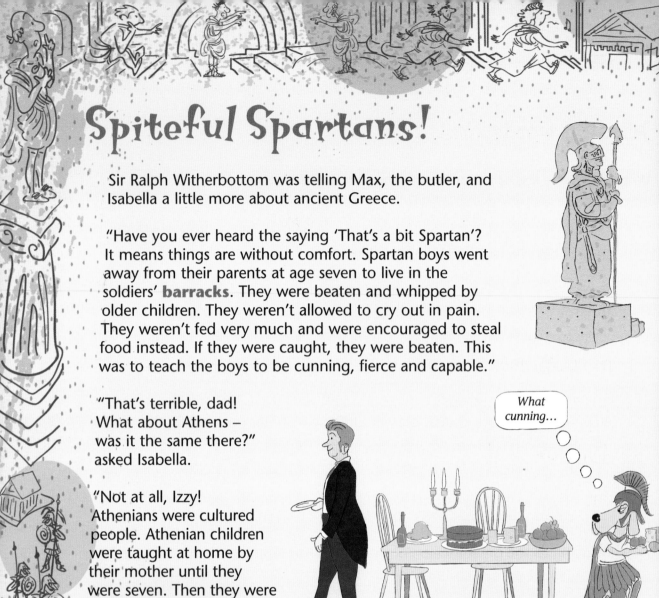

What cunning…

"Athenians valued being creative and polite, and they believed in **democracy**, where everyone has a say in what happens – but only if you were a **citizen**," said Sir Ralph.

"It says in this leaflet that the Spartans believed in equality of a sort, so they did have something in common with the Athenians! They believed that land should be divided equally among all people, and that people – rich and poor – should eat their meals together in large halls," said Max, the butler.

"Well, I for one would hate to be a Spartan, whether they ate together or not!" said Isabella.

Athenian or Spartan?

Write 'A' for Athenian or 'S' for Spartan in the boxes next to each statement.

1   They were taken away from their parents at age seven. `S`

2   They believed that land should be divided equally among all people. `S`

3   Their children were taught at home by their mothers. `A`

4   They were cultured people. `A`

5   They lived in the soldiers' barracks. `S`

6   They believed in democracy. `A`

7   They believed that rich and poor should eat their meals together in large halls. `S`

8   They were not fed much, and were encouraged to steal food. `S`

9   They were not allowed to cry out in pain. `S`

10 They learned drama, reading, writing, mathematics, public speaking and music. `A`

11 They were beaten and whipped by older children. `S`

Top Tips

Find out more about the Spartans by searching 'Spartans Greek' on the Internet. If you just type in 'Spartans' you get a lot of results about American sports!

Did you know?

Early Athens was ruled by **tyrants**. The Athenians invented **ostracism** to deal with tyrants. That means being cast out of society. Each person was allowed to ask for one person to be sent away from Athens. If enough people named the same person, he would be banished for ten years.

Armed and Dangerous!

Isabella Witherbottom, Max, the butler, and Sir Ralph went to a museum that displayed models of Greek soldiers in battle.

"Look, dad! It says here that the Greek army was made up of **volunteers**. No one had to be a soldier if they didn't want to. I know the Spartans were great fighters, but it sounds as though all the Greeks were pretty good at it!" said Isabella.

"Yes, they were, Izzy. The ancient Greeks went into battle, fighting in a line. They all held a shield that covered half of themselves and all of the man to their left. The whole army were forced to stick together, because if one soldier ran away, he would leave the rest unprotected. They all charged together, storming into their opponents," said Sir Ralph.

"They sound quite terrifying, dad! What sort of weapons did they carry?" asked Isabella.

"They carried a spear and a large shield. Some warriors carried short, vicious swords," said Sir Ralph. "Each soldier was called a **hoplite**, after the shield they carried, which was called a **hoplon**."

"What armour did they wear, dad?"

You watch my back, and I'll watch yours...

"They wore bronze and leather armour and a bronze helmet to protect themselves. The armour covered their whole body, except for the neck and groin. The helmets were made from metal and were heavy. In hot weather they got very hot and the poor men could become quite dehydrated!"

"Hmmm... I know how they feel! That reminds me, can we go and get a lolly now, dad?" joked Isabella.

Design a poster

Design a poster encouraging men to join the ancient Greek army – how will you persuade them? Use pictures of the great armour and weapons to help you to 'sell' the idea.

JOIN THE ARMY!

reasons to join the army.
- You'll become fit and strong.
- You'll know how to fight.
- You might make friends.

○ - sheild   ⚔ - sword   dagger

Top Tips

You can see what ancient Greek soldiers wore at the British Museum – if you cannot visit, look at the website at:
http://www.thebritishmuseum.ac.uk/

Did you know?

The Greeks did not have much 'fighting time' during the year. Their favourite **tactic** was to destroy a town by burning its crops. The fields would burn best in early September, so most of the fighting went on during this period; at other times it would be too wet, or the crops wouldn't have grown yet.

Revise Time

1 **Answer these questions about ancient Greece.**

a When were the first Olympic Games held? _776 BG_

b What does BC mean? _Before christ_

c Who wrote the Odyssey? _Homer_

d Who was the hero of the Odyssey? _Odysseus_

e Who wrote the Iliad? _Homerus_

f When were the Iliad and the Odyssey written? _750 BC_

2 **Fill in the missing letters.**

a _O_ ly _m_ _p_ ic

b O _d_ _y_ _s_ _s_ ey

c _H_ o _m_ e _r_

d I _l_ i _a_ d

e Br _o_ _n_ _z_ _e_ A _g_ e

f M _e_ _r_ m _a_ _i_ d

g An _c_ _i_ _e_ _n_ _t_ g _r_ ee _c_ _e_

h Ba _t_ _h_ s

3 **Fill in the missing words.**

a The _Spartans_ believed that everyone – rich and poor – should eat together.

b The _Athians_ believed in democracy.

c Athenians were _cultured_ people.

d _Athenians_ learned many different arts as part of their education.

e Spartan boys lived in the soldiers' _barracks_.

f Spartan boys were _encouraged_ to steal food.

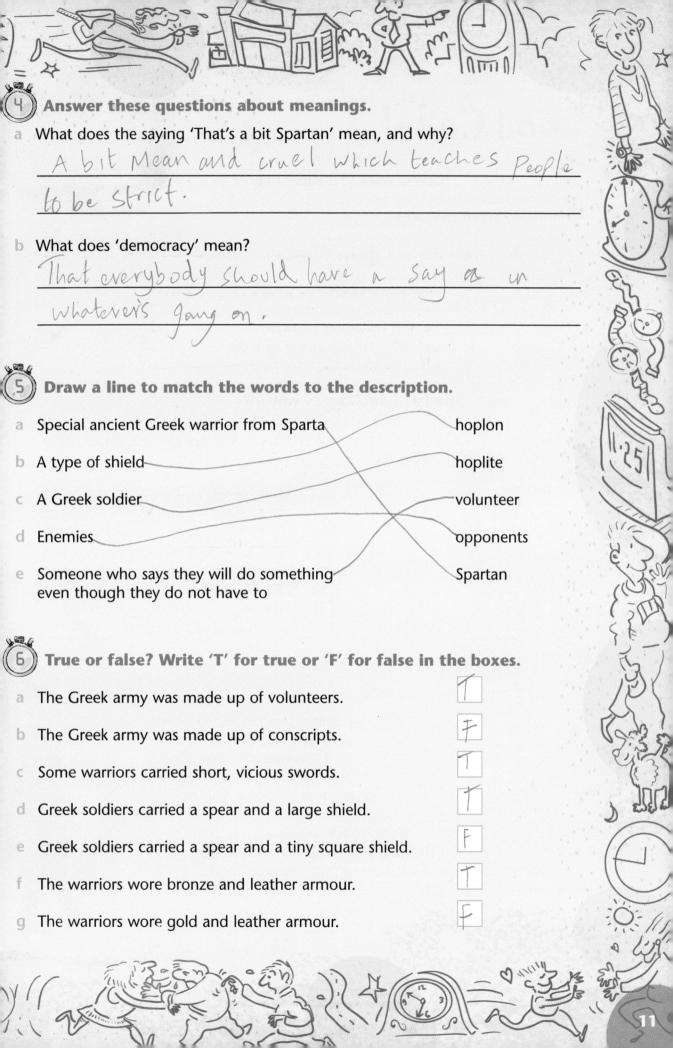

4 **Answer these questions about meanings.**

a What does the saying 'That's a bit Spartan' mean, and why?

A bit Mean and cruel which teaches People to be strict.

b What does 'democracy' mean?

That everybody should have a say a in whatever's going on.

5 **Draw a line to match the words to the description.**

a Special ancient Greek warrior from Sparta — hoplon

b A type of shield — hoplite

c A Greek soldier — volunteer

d Enemies — opponents

e Someone who says they will do something even though they do not have to — Spartan

6 **True or false? Write 'T' for true or 'F' for false in the boxes.**

a The Greek army was made up of volunteers. T

b The Greek army was made up of conscripts. F

c Some warriors carried short, vicious swords. T

d Greek soldiers carried a spear and a large shield. T

e Greek soldiers carried a spear and a tiny square shield. F

f The warriors wore bronze and leather armour. T

g The warriors wore gold and leather armour. F

11

Good Gods!

Sir Ralph, Max and Isabella went to a street market to find some souvenirs of their holiday. Isabella saw some brightly coloured **mosaics**.

"Look, dad – I like this one. It says 'Artemis'. Who was she?" asked Isabella.

"She was the ancient Greek moon goddess. She protected children and pregnant women. This one next to her is Aphrodite, the goddess of love.

"The ancient Greeks had many gods, you see, all with different 'jobs'. They believed that the gods lived on Mount Olympus, the highest mountain in Greece. Look – this one's called Zeus. He was the ruler of all the gods and his symbol was a thunderbolt, which he threw down to earth when he was cross!"

I'm a god among dogs!

"Who's this one, dad? He's got a trident like a mermaid!" said Isabella.

"That's Zeus's brother, Poseidon. He was the god of the sea. In an age when people could only travel around the world by sea, to upset Poseidon was a big mistake as he could destroy your boat with a giant wave!"

"Who's this dark god? He looks spooky!" said Isabella.

"Ah – that's Hades. He was the god of the underworld! And this one's Athene; Zeus's daughter. She was the goddess of wisdom and war. This god was called Apollo, god of sun, light, music and truth; and here's Hermes, the messenger of the gods. The ancient Greeks said he invented the alphabet and mathematics," said Max.

"Huh! He's got a lot to answer for, then!" grumbled Isabella.

Match them up

Match each Greek god to the correct description.

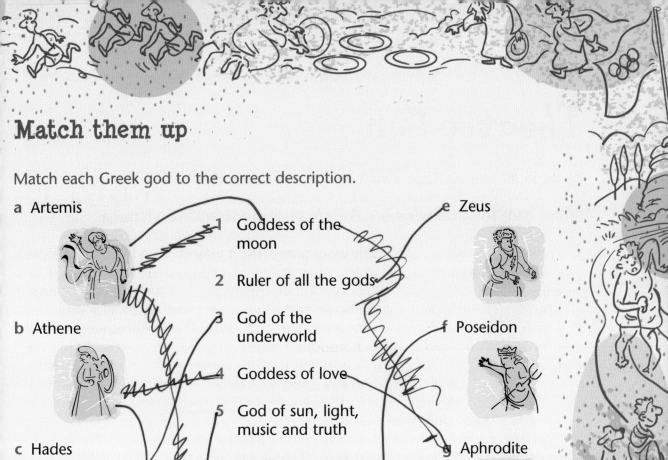

a Artemis

b Athene

c Hades

d Hermes

1 Goddess of the moon

2 Ruler of all the gods

3 God of the underworld

4 Goddess of love

5 God of sun, light, music and truth

6 Messenger of the gods – invented the alphabet and mathematics

7 God of the sea

8 Goddess of wisdom and war

e Zeus

f Poseidon

g Aphrodite

h Apollo

Top Tips

Find out more by reading 'The Orchard Book of Greek Gods and Goddesses', edited by Geraldine McCaughrean.

Did you know?

The ancient Greeks told bloodthirsty tales about their gods. Zeus was told that if he had a son, the child would destroy him, so when he found out that he was going to be a father, he swallowed pregnant Metis. Zeus got a terrible headache and ordered Hephaestus to split his skull with an axe. Athene jumped out of the split skull fully grown, armed and ready to fight!

Theatre Fun

Whilst in Athens, Sir Ralph took Isabella to see an ancient Greek theatre.

"Wow, dad! This theatre's more like a football **stadium**!" said Isabella.

"Isn't it amazing? The theatres were built on hillsides in the open air and could hold as many as 18,000 people! Greek theatres didn't have roofs, because it was warm in Greece for most of the year and people could sit outside. The theatres were built in a horseshoe shape with rows of stone seats in tiers, which meant that the whole of the audience had a great view," said Sir Ralph.

"And could hear everything well too," said Isabella. "This guidebook talks about the special **acoustics** of the theatres, which allowed the sound to travel to all parts of the theatre – clever stuff, isn't it, dad?" said Isabella.

"Absolutely! But you won't like this bit, Izzy. All the actors were men," Sir Ralph chuckled.

"What? How ridiculous!" grumbled Isabella.

"Strange, isn't it? The actors wore big masks…" began Sir Ralph.

"Ooh! I know this! The tragedy and comedy masks!" Isabella interrupted excitedly. "Greek plays were either comedies or tragedies. Tragedies were often about the past and comedies were usually about everyday life in the present."

"Well done, Izzy! So you do listen to me sometimes! Did you also know that the mouth hole on the masks was large for a reason? It was to **amplify** the voices of the actors," said Sir Ralph.

"Ah – so that's how my teacher manages to talk so loudly!" laughed Isabella.

Label it

Label the picture below using these descriptions.

> Horseshoe-shaped theatre   Hillside   Tragedy mask   Comedy mask
>
> Rows of stone seats   Special acoustics

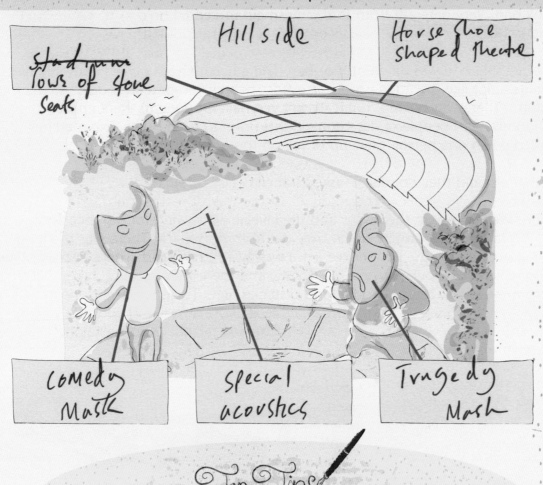

Hillside

Horse shoe shaped theatre

Stadium rows of stone seats

Comedy Mask

Special acoustics

Tragedy Mask

Top Tips

Make a 3D Greek theatre from a strip of card
bent into a semicircle, stuck onto a card base.
Add seats and actors!

Did you know?

Usually, ancient Greek actors wore masks made from **linen**, wood, or leather.
Human and animal hair was added to make details. The eyes were drawn on
the mask, but the pupils of the eyes were cut out so there were holes for the
actor to see through. Actors in comedies wore bright colours and actors in
tragedies wore dark colours.

Fun and Games

Sir Ralph, Max and Isabella visited a site where the Olympic Games had once been held.

"Hey, dad – it says in the guidebook that the original Olympic Games was a religious festival and only Greeks took part. Very different from the games held today!" said Isabella.

"Something else was different too, Izzy. The ancient Greek games had only nine events – not like the huge variety of events people compete in today!" said Sir Ralph. "There was boxing, but it wasn't very fair. Opponents were chosen randomly, with people of different weights fighting each other. The matches ended when one person gave up or fell on the ground!"

"What else did they do, dad?" asked Isabella.

"Well, they had the discus and the javelin – throwing for distance and throwing at a target, which they did from horseback. There was the long jump, where the jumper carried a weight in each hand. There was wrestling, which was similar to how it is today, and there were running races – 200 metres, 400 metres, and a long-distance race. There was even one in which athletes wore armour! Then there was **chariot** racing," said Sir Ralph.

May the best dog win!

"It says here that there was also a sport called **pankration**. It was a mixture of boxing and wrestling. It was really violent! There were two types. In the first, whoever fell on the ground first lost. In the second, whoever was knocked out first lost! Pankration athletes were often seriously injured or even died!" said Max.

Define the word

Design a programme telling a spectator at the Olympic Games in ancient Greece about the different events they will be watching. Include writing about pankration, javelin, discus, chariot racing and running races.

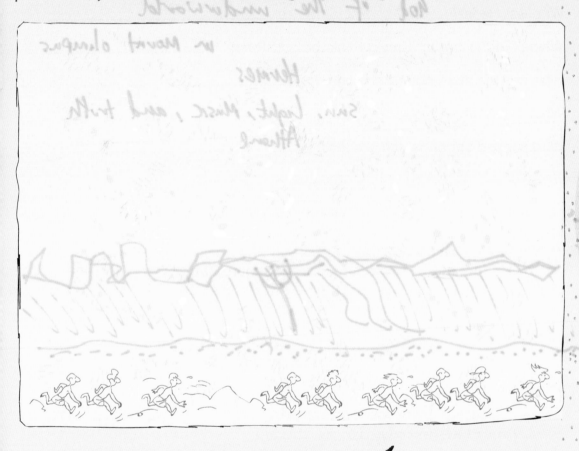

Top Tips!
Look on the Internet to find out more about the similarities and differences between the Olympics now and in ancient Greece.
http://www.perseus.tufts.edu/Olympics/sports.html

Did you know?
The throwers of the discus originally threw a circular stone and then later a circular shape made of iron, lead, or bronze. The movements and techniques of ancient discus throwers were very similar to those of today's athletes.

Revise Time

1 Answer these questions about the Greek gods.

a Who was the Greek goddess of love? ~~Athene~~ Aphrodite

b Who was Hades? god of the underworld

c Where did the ancient Greeks think the gods lived? in Mount olimpus

d Who was the messenger of the gods? Hermes

e What was Apollo the god of? Sun, light, Music, and truth

f Who popped out of her father's skull? Athene

2 Draw a picture of the underworld as you imagine it in the box below.

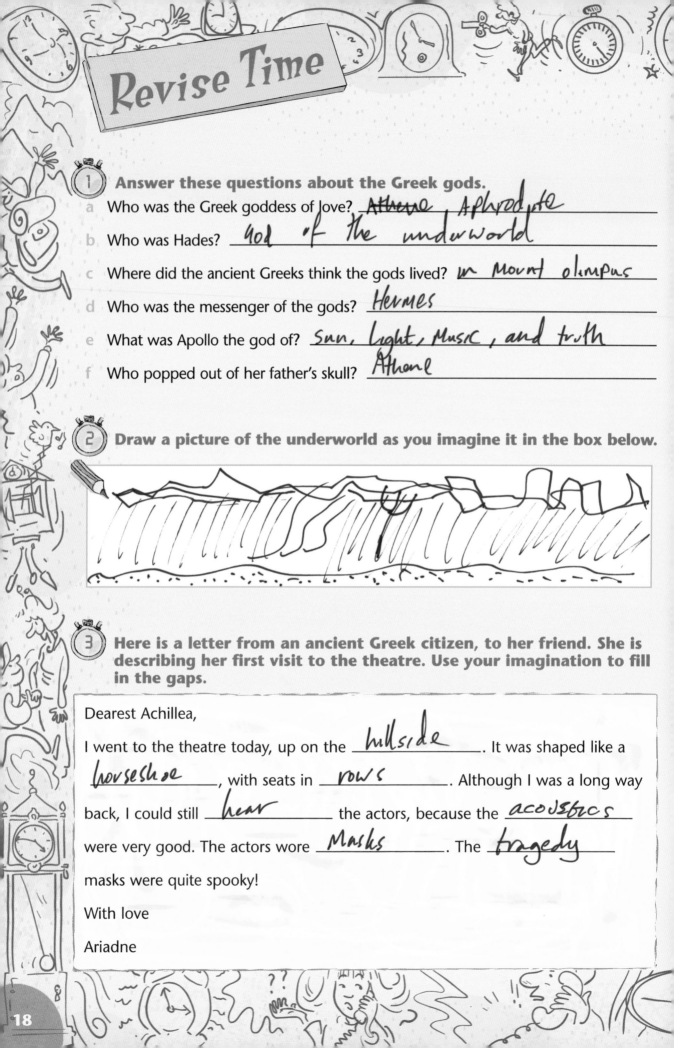

3 Here is a letter from an ancient Greek citizen, to her friend. She is describing her first visit to the theatre. Use your imagination to fill in the gaps.

Dearest Achillea,

I went to the theatre today, up on the _hillside_. It was shaped like a _horseshoe_, with seats in _rows_. Although I was a long way back, I could still _hear_ the actors, because the _acoustics_ were very good. The actors wore _Masks_. The _tragedy_ masks were quite spooky!

With love

Ariadne

18

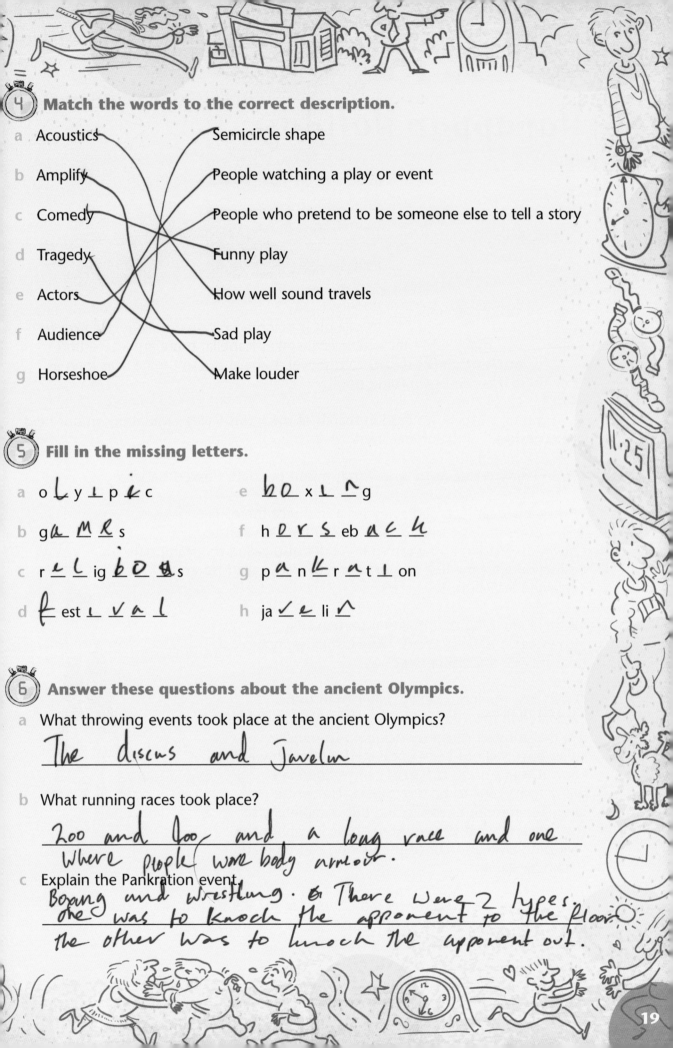

4 Match the words to the correct description.

a Acoustics — How well sound travels

b Amplify — Sad play

c Comedy — People who pretend to be someone else to tell a story

d Tragedy — Make louder

e Actors — Semicircle shape

f Audience — People watching a play or event

g Horseshoe — Funny play

Semicircle shape

People watching a play or event

People who pretend to be someone else to tell a story

Funny play

How well sound travels

Sad play

Make louder

5 Fill in the missing letters.

a o L y _ p i c

b g a M e s

c r e l ig i o u s

d f est i v a l

e b o x i n g

f h o r s eb a c k

g p a n k r a t i on

h ja v e li n

6 Answer these questions about the ancient Olympics.

a What throwing events took place at the ancient Olympics?

The discus and Javelin

b What running races took place?

200 and 400 and a long race and one
where people wore body armour.

c Explain the Pankration event.

Boxing and wrestling. There were 2 types.
one was to knock the opponent to the floor
the other was to knock the opponent out.

19

Harappan Holiday

Sir Ralph is planning his next holiday. He likes to make sure that wherever he takes Isabella, there are interesting **ancient civilisations** to discover. Isabella doesn't mind – as long as there is a good swimming pool!

"Hmmm… I think we'll go in search of the Indus valley civilisation on our next **excursion**!" Sir Ralph declared.

"Can I have a clue as to where that might be, dad?" asked Isabella.

"Sorry, my dear – carried away for a moment there! The Indus valley civilisation flourished around 2500 BC in what today is known as Pakistan and western India. It's also called the Harappan civilisation after the first city to be discovered, called Harappa," explained Sir Ralph.

> Let's get cracking!

"Is there anything that makes it particularly interesting?" Isabella asked. "Any lost cities, hoards of treasure – or ancient curses?"

"Well, Izzy, the Indus valley only began to be excavated in the 1920s. The exciting thing about it is that most of its ruins, including its major cities, have still not been excavated. Although we know it was a great **cultural** centre, there are many secrets still to be discovered. The written language has not been worked out completely, so just imagine what the world might learn about this amazing civilisation once the writing can be read!" said Sir Ralph.

"A mystery! Well, why didn't you say so? It'll be just like 'Indiana Jones'! I hope we don't get squashed by any traps in ancient tombs though…!" joked Isabella.

Wordsearch

Find the words hidden in the wordsearch.

tombs · excavated · cultural · civilisation · Indus

Harappa · ancient · excursion

i	n	d	u	s	e	s	b	v	w	c	h
t	t	n	o	i	s	r	u	c	x	e	b
o	o	u	n	t	r	l	s	s	d	a	a
m	c	u	l	t	u	r	a	l	x	r	n
b	e	x	c	a	v	a	t	e	d	t	c
s	e	n	a	l	w	m	z	k	w	s	i
c	b	m	w	e	c	t	k	i	p	c	e
c	i	v	i	l	i	s	a	t	i	o	n
h	e	a	d	a	p	p	a	r	a	h	t

Top Tips

You can find exactly where the Indus valley civilisation
was, on a map of the ancient world at the library.

Did you know?

The Indus valley civilisation covered a huge area. There were about 1000
settlements and the remains of these settlements have been found across
most of modern Pakistan, parts of the north-west of India and northern
Afghanistan. Remains of the Indus valley civilisation are found across one
of the largest geographical areas covered by any single Bronze Age culture.

Long Ago and Far Away

Isabella wanted to find out more about the Indus valley civilisation, so she took down a history book from the bookshelf in the study.

"It says here, dad, that the Indus valley civilisation was the earliest known civilisation in India. Apparently, from the beginning of the fourth **millennium** BC, small villages could be found in the area. Eventually, 1500 Indus valley settlements were scattered over 280,000 square miles. From around 3000 BC there were larger settlements and cities. It says that in 2200 BC, the city of Harappa covered 370 acres and 80,000 people lived there!" said Isabella. "That would make it from the same time period as Egypt's earliest pyramids and the great civilisations of **Mesopotamia**! Just think, in Britain at the same time, the great stone circle at Stonehenge was being built."

"Yes, Izzy – I find the ancient world fascinating, as you know, and Harappa is a truly ancient city. It was built on the **fertile** coastal plain and it was about the same size as the great city of Ur in Mesopotamia. The Indus valley civilisation was peaceful and **prosperous**. Harappa was a great trading centre, found on the crossroads of many of the great trade routes. Just imagine the rich **merchants** with their caravans of camels, trekking across the desert…so romantic…"

This is really giving me the hump.

"And so smelly…yuck! I remember the camels we rode on holiday last year. I'd rather use a real caravan, thanks!" laughed Isabella.

Your number's up

Fill in the blanks with the correct number.

1 In the _____ millennium BC, small villages could be found all over the Indus valley.

2 Around _____ BC, larger settlements and cities appeared.

3 By _____ BC, the city of Harappa was a large settlement.

4 Harappa covered _____ acres.

5 Around _____ people lived in Harappa.

6 Eventually, there were _____ Indus valley settlements.

7 These settlements were spread out over _____ square miles.

terracotta figurine

Top Tips

Look for cities in the UK with a population of 80,000 to give you an idea of the size of Harappa.

Did you know?

Through trade, the Indus valley civilisation came into contact with faraway lands. People from the Indus valley travelled along the coast and the rivers as well as on the roads. **Archaeologists** have found many imported goods including gold and jade from India, copper from Afghanistan and turquoise from Iran. Indus pottery has been discovered at many ancient sites too.

Exciting Excavations!

Isabella typed 'Indus Valley' into a search engine on the Internet. She found lots of sites with pictures of the **excavations**.

"Look, Max! It says on this site that when the great railway linking Lahore to Multan in Pakistan was being built in 1856, the builders smashed through the remains of what they thought was an old Buddhist temple. It was Harappa, one of the greatest cities of the Indus valley civilisation!" said Isabella.

"I bet nothing that exciting was found when our local station was built, Izzy!" laughed Max.

"Then, it says, in the 1870s, the archaeologist Sir Alexander Cunningham found a small seal, used for putting a mark on messages. Pottery **fragments** were found at the site too. These finds were to lead to the first real detailed excavations by Rai Bahadur Daya Ram Sahni. In 1920, many beautifully engraved seals were found. Rakhal Das Banerji also began excavations at another Indus valley site called Mohenjo-Daro. He found many objects and the remains of another huge city."

Seals?
In the desert?

"Yes, I've read something about this, Izzy. The excavations carried on during the 1920s and 1930s, with several teams of archaeologists. The excavations stopped around 1935 and didn't start again until 1950. Sir Mortimer Wheeler used modern archaeological methods to look at new discoveries – and to reinterpret some of the earlier finds too."

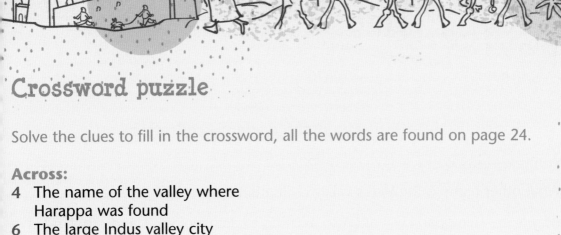

Crossword puzzle

Solve the clues to fill in the crossword, all the words are found on page 24.

Across:

4 The name of the valley where Harappa was found
6 The large Indus valley city
8 A dig carried out by archaeologists may be called this
9 Made from clay
10 Things found by archaeologists, left behind by ancient civilisations, such as buildings, etc

Down:

1 The great railway linked Lahore to this place
2 An Indus valley city beginning with the letter 'M'
3 Used for putting a mark on messages
5 The finding of a site or artefact
7 Name of modern country where many Indus valley settlement remains have been found

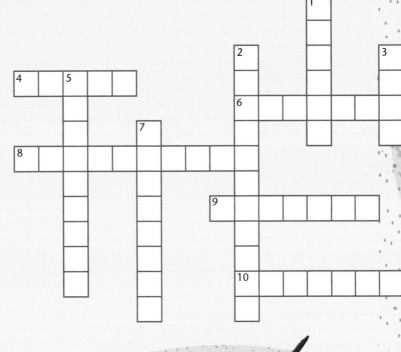

Top Tips

Use the Internet and books to investigate what people thought they had found when they built the railways in Victorian times.

Did you know?

Since 1986, the joint Pakistani and American Harappa Archaeological Research Project (HARP) has been carrying out excavations at Harappa. Archaeologists have found many pieces of pottery, marked with the writing common on Indus valley civilisation items. The archaeological team at Harappa includes archaeobotanists – experts in the study of plant remains from archaeological sites – and specialists in animal remains, and ancient technology.

Revise Time

1 Answer these questions about the ancient civilisations.

a Where was the Indus valley civilisation? _____

b What other name is the Indus valley civilisation known by? _____

c Why is the Harappan civilisation so exciting to archaeologists and scholars?

_____

d What needs to be done, for scholars to learn more about this civilisation?

_____

2 What do these words mean? Use the glossary or a dictionary to help you find the meanings.

a Ancient   _____

b Civilisation   _____

c Flourished   _____

d Excursion   _____

e Hoard   _____

f Cultural   _____

3 Answer these questions about the ancient civilisations.

a Which was the earliest known Indian civilisation? _____

b How many settlements were found? _____

c What was happening in Egypt at the time of the Harappan civilisation?

_____

d What was happening in Britain at the time of the Harappan civilisation?

_____

e Which great city in Mesopotamia was around the same size as Harappa?

_____

f How many people lived in Harappa when it was at its height? _____

4) Fill in the missing words.

a   Harappa was built on a fertile _____ plain.

b   The Indus valley civilisation was peaceful and _____.

c   From the beginning of the fourth _____ BC, small villages could be found all over the Indus valley.

d   Eventually 1500 Indus valley _____ were scattered over 280,000 square miles.

e   The Indus valley _____ was the earliest known civilisation in India.

f   Harappa was a thriving city in the same time period as Egypt's earliest _____ were being built.

5) True or false? Write 'T' for true or 'F' for false in the boxes.

a   Rakhal Das Banerji carried out excavations at Mohenjo-Daro.

b   In the 1970s, Sir Alexander Cunningham found a small seal.

c   When the Lahore to Multan railway was being built, the builders smashed through the remains of what they thought was an old Buddhist temple.

d   In 1820, many beautifully engraved seals were found.

e   The ruins were Harappa, one of the greatest cities of the Indus valley civilisation.

f   Rakhal Das Banerji found few objects at the excavation site.

6) Fill in the missing letters.

a   Re _ _ _ ns

b   _ _ ddhis _

c   Ex _ _ _ _ _ ions

d   S _ a _ _

e   P _ _ _ ery

f   Fr _ _ _ _ _ ts

g   Ar _ _ _ _ _ ol _ _ ist

A Tale of Two Cities

Sir Ralph and Max took Isabella to the museum to see an exhibition about the Indus valley civilisations.

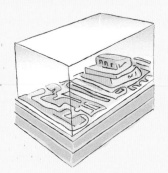

"Look, dad – a model of Mohenjo-Daro! It was a well planned town, wasn't it? I'm surprised that it was laid out in such a rectangular pattern, though. It looks like it was all built at once, rather than bit by bit over time!"

"Ah, yes, Izzy. The city was exceptionally well planned. The houses were made from burnt brick and stone, like they were in Harappa. It had a great **drainage** system, sewers, wells and water storage systems. The houses were built on two storeys, and even had bathrooms, with washing platforms and lavatories!" said Sir Ralph.

"The model shows the eastern part of the city. It says it was known as the Lower Town. Archaeologists believe that most people lived and worked in the Lower Town. It's incredible to find out so much about life in the past from what people left behind, isn't it, dad?" said Isabella.

I don't care if you are an archaeologist – go away!

"I think it's wonderful, Izzy! I love the broad streets they had in Mohenjo-Daro. They put our congested town to shame!" said Sir Ralph.

"What are these, dad?" asked Isabella.

"They're **granaries**, which were storehouses for the whole community. Have you noticed that there's no large house that looks like a palace? Perhaps Mohenjo-Daro didn't have an **emperor** or other ruler! You can work out some amazing things from archaeological digs!"

Word scramble

Unscramble these words.

1 nasriegra _____

2 mmuncoity _____

3 eroremp _____

4 appahar _____

5 summeu _____

6 iduns _____

7 gaindrea _____

8 souhse _____

9 lapcae _____

10 nashwig _____

Top Tips

Have a look at the book 'Indus Valley City'
by Gillian Clements to find out more.

Did you know?

In Harappa, the drains started from the bathrooms of the houses and
travelled out to join the main sewer in the street in a similar way to today.
That was amazingly sophisticated! The sewer was covered by stone slabs to
keep it sealed and this kept the streets clean and healthy.

Artful Artisans

Isabella, Max and Sir Ralph were watching a film presentation about the Indus valley civilisation and the farmers and traders of Mohenjo-Daro.

"Look at that beautiful jewellery and those complex game pieces, all made from precious stones, and those toys, too!" said Sir Ralph.

"I like that monkey that slides down a string – it looks quite modern, really! It's amazing to think a child was playing with it over 2000 years ago!" said Isabella.

"That's right, Izzy! Actually, many **artisans** worked in Mohenjo-Daro. Objects made from copper, bronze and pottery have been found, including many **terracotta** toys. Beads made from precious stones were found, too. The holes through the middle were regular and had been made with tiny drills. This shows that technology in Mohenjo-Daro was quite advanced," said Sir Ralph. "Goods were also brought in from far away to be traded in Mohenjo-Daro."

"Like copper, tin and lapis lazuli from Afghanistan; clams and conches from the coast; timber from the Himalayas; semi-precious stones from Gujarat; and silver and gold from central Asia," Isabella interrupted proudly. "Artisans then made the materials into goods which they traded with Mesopotamia, Iran and central Asia."

"What a good memory you have, Izzy! If only you could remember to tidy your room once in a while!" laughed Max.

Gold and gems I can understand – but tin?

Circle the items

Draw a circle round the artefacts that may have been found in the Indus valley excavations. Then give a reason why the objects you have not chosen could not have been found there.

_____

_____

_____

Top Tips!

Look at modern semi-precious beads.
How do you think the hole through the
middle has been made?

Did you know?

Seals carved with crocodiles, rhinos and other animals were found at Mohenjo-Daro. Archaeologists believe that these were **symbols** of different families or clans. Seals with carvings of unicorns were found too – and they were the earliest pictures of unicorns ever found. Some of the seals are carved from semi-precious stones and are very beautiful.

Bathtime Bliss

Sir Ralph had bought Isabella a book about Mohenjo-Daro. It had lots of pictures of the town, including the Great Bath. She was looking through it with Max.

"Look at this, Max! Archaeologists discovered a Great Bath at Mohenjo-Daro, which was 12 metres long and 7 metres wide. It was nearly 2 metres deep. It was made waterproof with a layer of sticky **bitumen**. Around the edges of the Great Bath there were small changing rooms on three sides, smaller baths and a covered walkway called a cloister. Why would they have public baths in Mohenjo-Daro when they all had washing platforms at home?"

"Well, Izzy, they did have bathrooms at home for washing – an amazing technological triumph for the ancient world – but perhaps the public baths weren't really for washing in! Archaeologists think that the public baths at Mohenjo-Daro may have been a meeting place or even a place of worship," said Max.

"How could baths be a place of worship?" asked Isabella. "That seems a bit unlikely!"

"Well, Izzy, many religions even today have a 'ritual of purification', where water is used as a symbol – Hindu, Jewish and Christian people all use water as a part of worship," said Max.

"Oh, I see! I must say I've never seen anyone saying their prayers at the swimming baths in town… unless they're going down the 'Deathly Drop' slide, that is!" Isabella laughed.

Lord help me!

Wordsearch

Find the words hidden in the wordsearch.

bath   waterproof   bitumen   changing   cloister   worship   purification   religion

b	i	t	u	m	e	n	b	v	w	c	h
a	t	e	e	n	p	i	h	s	r	o	w
t	o	u	n	t	r	l	s	s	d	a	d
h	d	u	n	o	i	g	i	l	e	r	x
b	e	n	a	c	u	a	t	e	d	t	v
s	e	n	c	l	o	i	s	t	e	r	a
c	h	a	n	g	i	n	g	i	s	c	a
p	u	r	i	f	i	c	a	t	i	o	n
h	e	f	o	o	r	p	r	e	t	a	w

Top Tips

Check out The Indus Valley
(Excavating the Past) series by
Ilona Aronovsky and Sujata
Gopinath.

Did you know?

Mohenjo-Daro has been on the **UNESCO World Heritage Site list** since
1980 – and it's no wonder, looking at its engineering! There are 40 oval-
shaped wells at the site – oval so that several people can draw water at the
same time. Fresh water enters the Great Bath via a well and dirty water runs
out via an efficient drainage system.

Revise Time

1 **Answer these questions about Harappa and Mohenjo-Daro.**

a What were the Harappan houses made from? _____

b Where was the Lower Town in Mohenjo-Daro? _____

c Where did most people work in the town of Harappa?

_____

d Was there a palace in Mohenjo-Daro? _____

e How many storeys did the houses have in Mohenjo-Daro? _____

2 **Write a short description of each of these things.**

a The houses in Mohenjo-Daro.

_____

b The bathrooms in Mohenjo-Daro.

_____

c The water system in Mohenjo-Daro.

_____

d The granaries in Mohenjo-Daro.

_____

3 **Tick the objects found at the dig at Mohenjo-Daro.**

a Plastic spoon ☐   e Polystyrene packaging ☐

b Pottery fragments ☐   f Gold jewellery ☐

c Terracotta toys ☐   g Silver jewellery ☐

d Precious stones ☐   h Watch ☐

4 Fill in the missing words.

a Many religions have a 'ritual of _____'.

b The public baths at Mohenjo-Daro may have been a place of _____.

c The Great Bath had small _____ rooms on three sides.

d The Great Bath was nearly 2 metres _____.

e Indus valley houses had bathrooms, which was an amazing technological triumph for the _____ world.

5 Answer these questions about the Great Bath.

a How was the Great Bath made waterproof?

_____

b What do archaeologists think the Great Bath may have been used for?

_____

6 Draw a sketch of the layout of the Great Bath, as described on page 32.

It's a Puzzle!

Sir Ralph showed Isabella a magazine that illustrated many different types of ancient writing. "Look, Izzy – my magazine shows the writing found in the Indus valley excavations. It may well be the earliest examples of writing! People in the Indus valley civilisation used a writing system based around pictures. It was used for several hundred years," said Sir Ralph.

"Like hieroglyphs from ancient Egypt? I liked working them out!" said Isabella.

I would say 'It's all Greek to me' – but then it isn't, is it?!

"They were similar, but unfortunately, so far, no one has been able to read the writing. The earliest examples seem to be scratched on jars, but whether the pictures talk about the contents, or whether they are dedications to the gods, nobody knows! With hieroglyphics, people were able to **decipher** hieroglyphs after the discovery of the Rosetta Stone. It was a huge piece of black rock, called basalt, which had writing carved on the face. The writing showed hieroglyphs and the corresponding Greek words. Scholars could read Greek already, so they were able to work out what the hieroglyphs meant too!" said Sir Ralph.

"Wow – there's a job for you, dad! It's a real mystery!" said Isabella.

"I think I'll leave it to the experts, such as the great Indian scholar Iratham Mahadevan and the archaeologist Dr Ahmad Hassan Dani. They've spent years examining the text and haven't come up with an answer. If they can't do it, I don't think I'd be able to!" chuckled Sir Ralph.

Write a message

People in the Indus valley used a series of symbols to write things down. These are not their symbols, but you can use them to write a message.

a h o v

b i p w

c j q x

d k r y

e l s z

f m t

g n u

Write 'Indus valley civilisation' in symbols in the box below.

Top Tips!

Look for other systems of writing that use symbols, such as Anglo-Saxon runes and ancient Egyptian hieroglyphs.

Did you know?

There are about 370 separate symbols in the Indus valley writing system. About 135 of these are found regularly. There are no surviving long documents, which makes the meaning of the writing hard to work out. This lack may be because people wrote on materials that have rotted away, such as bark, palm leaves or cotton.

You're History

Sir Ralph, Max and Isabella are eating lunch at a café in town.

"Dad, all the things you've shown me and told me about have made me think I'd like to be a historian or an archaeologist when I grow up," said Isabella.

"That's wonderful, my dear! What an interesting life you'd have!" said Sir Ralph. "You're very good at asking questions and that's a key skill for a historian."

"My teacher says we should be 'best friends' with the words 'who', 'what', 'where' and 'when'!" laughed Isabella.

"She's right, but historians need to think about 'why' and 'how' even more often!" said Sir Ralph. "Historical research isn't just finding out facts, such as what happened when and where – it's more to do with finding out why things happened, and how events followed on from one another. It's like working out clues and putting a puzzle together."

"That's what makes it all so interesting!" said Isabella. "I like museums too. I especially like the displays about everyday life in the past and seeing how people lived in other **civilisations** through history. Looking at the artefacts, I can imagine that I'm a **suffragette**, a Celtic warrior queen, a roman slave or a Tudor lady – it's such great fun! Imagine what it would be like to be a historian and handle the things in the museum cases...or to be an archaeologist and actually discover the things that get displayed in museums...amazing!"

If you ask me, those historians should stop living in the past.

Write a list

Help Isabella make a list of all the reasons why being a historian or archaeologist would be fun. Use her ideas from the introduction and think of some more of your own!

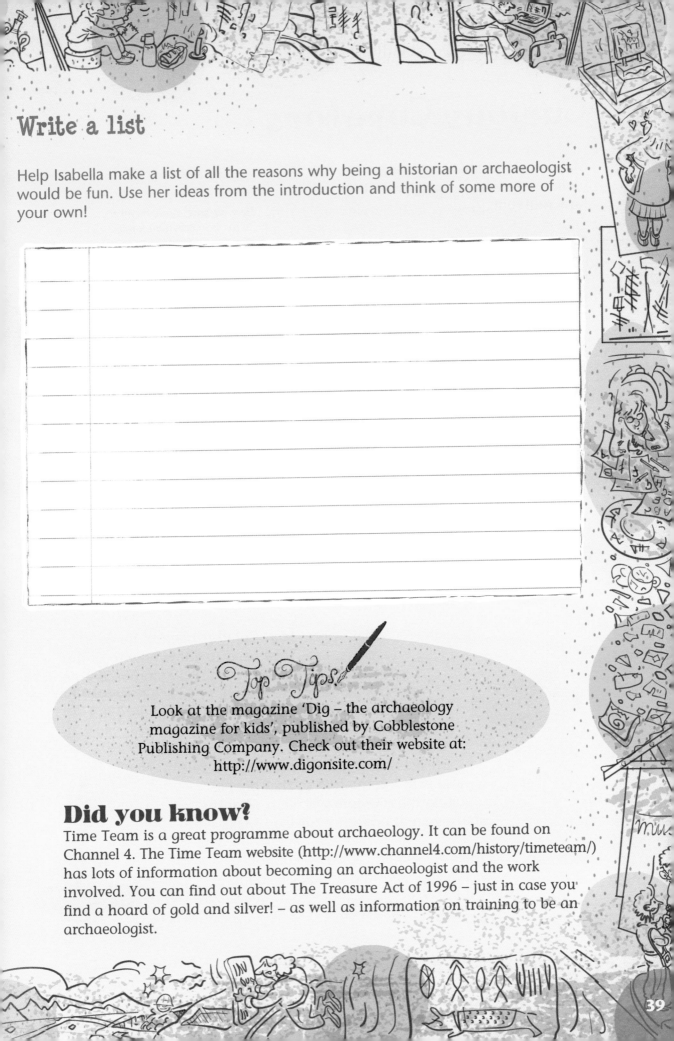

Top Tips

Look at the magazine 'Dig – the archaeology magazine for kids', published by Cobblestone Publishing Company. Check out their website at: http://www.digonsite.com/

Did you know?

Time Team is a great programme about archaeology. It can be found on Channel 4. The Time Team website (http://www.channel4.com/history/timeteam/) has lots of information about becoming an archaeologist and the work involved. You can find out about The Treasure Act of 1996 – just in case you find a hoard of gold and silver! – as well as information on training to be an archaeologist.

Curious Curators

Max is taking Isabella to meet a friend of his who is a **curator** at the local museum.

Here we have a rare member of the Witherbottom family.

"If you talk to my friend Sophie, you can find out more about the types of work historians carry out. She spends lots of time **conserving** objects for the museum, so that they're preserved for years to come and can be **exhibited** and studied safely," said Max.

He gave Isabella a leaflet sent to him by his friend to give to her. "Listen, Max, it says here that **conservators** and conservation scientists help to store and display historical artefacts in the correct conditions to stop them from **deteriorating**. It says artefacts often need to be cleaned, restored and even reconstructed. It must be like a huge jigsaw puzzle at times!" said Isabella.

"That's right, Izzy! Curators need to be good teachers, too. They need to know how to group artefacts together according to a common theme, such as how the items were used, or where they are from, so that people will see connections and understand more about different time periods in history. Then they need to be able to label the artefacts – not just with the names, but also with information so that people visiting the museum will learn what the items were used for," explained Max.

"I think we should call you a curator, Max. You look after old things, like dad!" laughed Isabella.

Word scramble

Unscramble these words.

1 urcator _____

2 usemum _____

3 bitexhi _____

4 servingcon _____

5 structedrecon _____

6 storyhi _____

7 fteactsar _____

8 sawgji _____

9 leandec _____

10 storreed _____

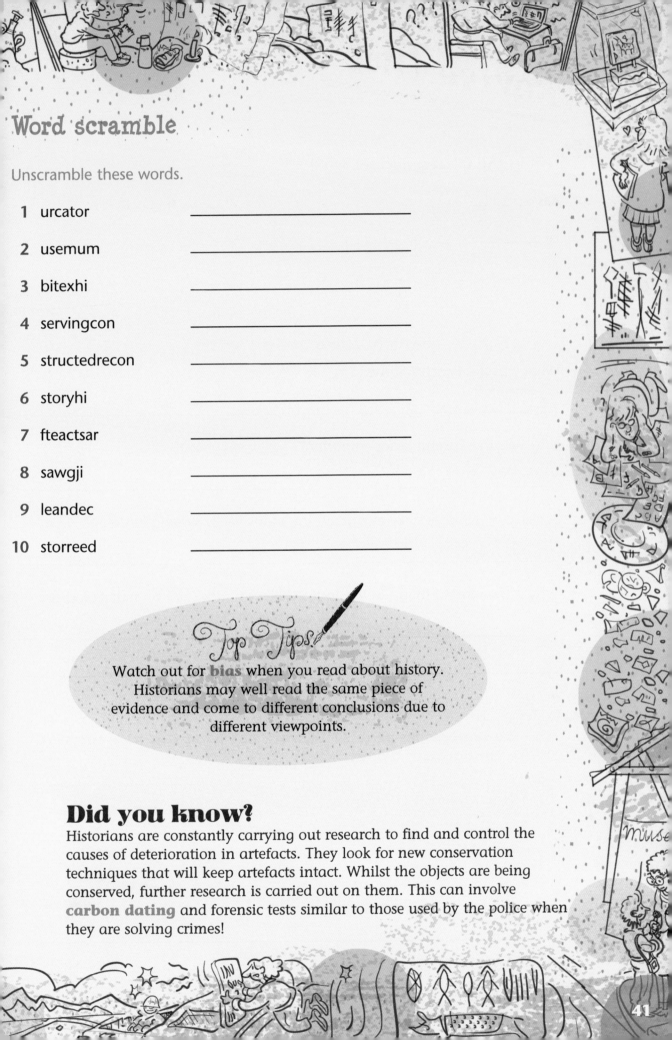

Top Tips

Watch out for **bias** when you read about history. Historians may well read the same piece of evidence and come to different conclusions due to different viewpoints.

Did you know?

Historians are constantly carrying out research to find and control the causes of deterioration in artefacts. They look for new conservation techniques that will keep artefacts intact. Whilst the objects are being conserved, further research is carried out on them. This can involve **carbon dating** and forensic tests similar to those used by the police when they are solving crimes!

Revise Time

1 **Fill in the missing letters.**

a Bas __ __ __

b Hi __ __ __ __ __ yph __ __s

c Ro __ __ __ __ __   __ __ __ __ e

d W __ __ ti __ __

e Sc __ __ __ __ r

2 **Answer these questions about ancient writing.**

a What was the Rosetta Stone?

_____

b Why was the Rosetta Stone important?

_____

c Which two scholars have examined the Indus valley writing in detail?

_____   _____

d Why is the writing found in the Indus valley so important to archaeologists?

_____

_____

3 **Use the symbols on page 37 to work out what this message says. Write your answer below.**

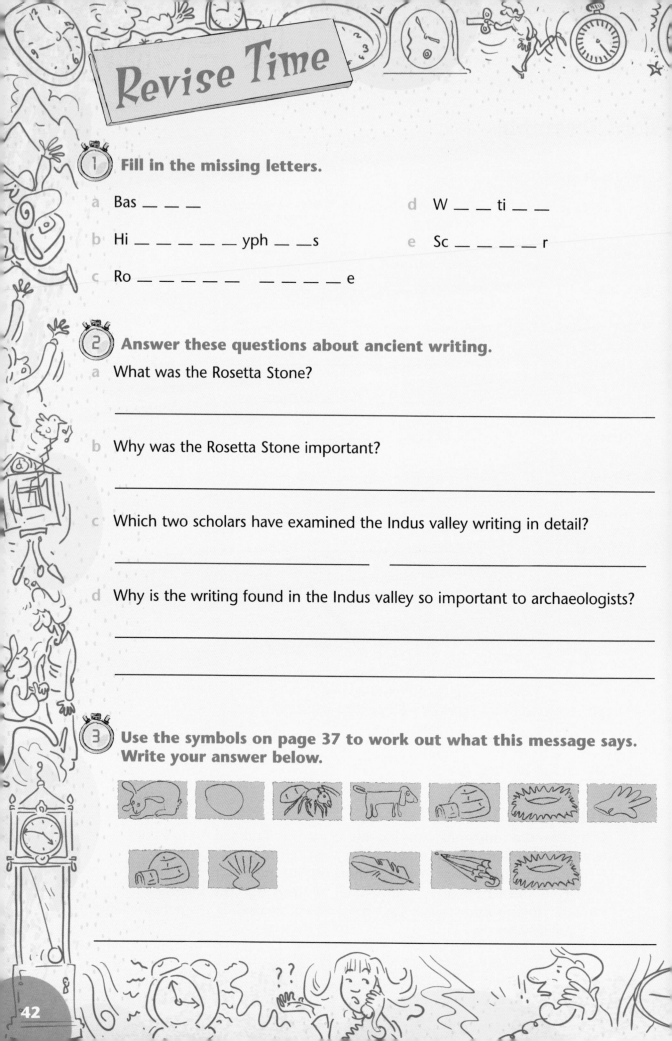

_____

42

4 **Write a description of the work done by:**

a   A historian. _____

_____

b   An archaeologist. _____

_____

5 **What do these words mean? Use the glossary or a dictionary to help you.**

a   Curator   _____

b   Conserve   _____

c   Exhibit   _____

d   Museum   _____

e   Artefact   _____

f   Bias   _____

g   Deterioration   _____

6 **Write a job description for a museum curator. Make it sound exciting!**

_____

_____

_____

_____

_____

_____

_____

43

Glossary

acoustics how well things sound and are heard

amplify to increase the strength of something, such as sound

ancient very old; ancient history is from the times of the Greeks, Egyptians, Indus valley civilisations etc.

archaeologist a person who looks for evidence of life in the past

artisans skilled workers who make things

barracks where soldiers live

BC the period of time 'before Christ'

bias when someone has a particular viewpoint and it clouds the way they think, we say they are biased

bitumen tar used to make roads

Bronze Age a period in history before iron was introduced when most tools and weapons were made from bronze

carbon dating a method of finding out how old something is

chariot ancient war 'cart' pulled by horses

citizen a person who is a member of a particular civilisation

civilisation a system people have created and live in, such as the Indus valley

conservators people who preserve things; usually historical artefacts

conserving preserving things

cultural having an interest in the arts – literature, music, etc

culture the artistic activities and ideas that belong to a particular time and place

curator a person who looks after and conserves items and artefacts in a museum

decipher to work something out

democracy where everyone in a community has a say in what happens and the people or their representatives make decisions

deteriorating when the condition or state of something gets worse over time

drainage a system for taking away waste water

emperor a type of ruler; similar to a king

excavations where earth is dug away to find remains and artefacts

excursion a trip

exhibited shown; an exhibition in a museum is a display of items

fertile able to produce a lot of something, such as vegetation or crops

fragments pieces

granaries storage for grain, often for the whole community

hoplite an ancient Greek soldier

hoplon a shield carried by an ancient Greek soldier

Iliad a series of stories written by Homer

linen material made from flax

merchants people who buy and sell things

Mesopotamia the area today is modern Iraq and part of Syria. Ancient Mesopotamia had a sophisticated, successful civilisation. The great city of Babylon, with its hanging gardens, was part of Mesopotamia

millennium a period of 1000 years

mosaic a picture made from small pieces of glass, stones etc.

Odyssey a series of stories written by Homer; the adventures of Odysseus

ostracism when someone is shut out from a society or group

pankration a mixture of wrestling and boxing from ancient Greece

prosperous wealthy and successful

ruins broken-down buildings

settlements where people decide to live and build houses and towns

stadium a place where people collect to watch sporting events

suffragette a woman who fought and campaigned for women to get the right to vote

symbols signs that mean something

tactic a plan for doing something, such as a battle

terracotta an orange material made from clay; used for making pots and crockery

tyrant a ruler, usually cruel, who allows no disagreement with his or her views

UNESCO World Heritage Site list a list of places with particular importance for the whole world, such as the Great Barrier Reef in Australia, the pyramids in Egypt, Kew Gardens in the UK, the Great Wall of China, and the Taj Mahal in India. UNESCO means 'United Nations Educational, Scientific and Cultural Organisation'

volunteer somebody who offers to do something, often without payment

Answers

Page 5
1 sophisticated
2 776 BC
3 Odyssey, Iliad
4 Bronze Age
5 Public baths
6 Before Christ

Page 7
1 S 2 S 3 A 4 A 5 S 6 A
7 S 8 S 9 S 10 A 11 S

Page 9
An appropriate poster encouraging men to join the army.

Pages 10–11 Revision exercises
Exercise 1
a 776 BC
b Before Christ
c Homer
d Odysseus
e Homer
f 750 BC

Exercise 2
a Olympic
b Odyssey
c Homer
d Iliad
e Bronze Age
f Mermaid
g Ancient Greece
h Baths

Exercise 3
a Spartans
b Athenians
c cultured
d Athenians
e barracks
f encouraged

Exercise 4
Many answers are appropriate. Some examples are:
a 'That's a bit Spartan' means without comfort. Spartans believed that a life without comfort made boys grow up to be fierce soldiers.
b Democracy is when everyone has a say in what happens and how society works.

Exercise 5
a Spartan
b hoplon
c hoplite
d opponents
e volunteer

Exercise 6
a T b F c T d T e F f T g F

Page 13
1 a 2 e 3 c 4 g 5 h 6 d
7 f 8 b

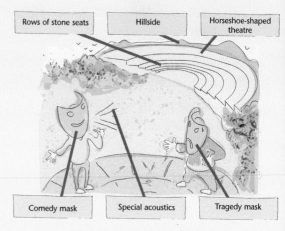

Rows of stone seats | Hillside | Horseshoe-shaped theatre

Comedy mask | Special acoustics | Tragedy mask

Page 17
Any suitable programme including details of the different events mentioned in the text.

Pages 18–19 Revision exercises
Exercise 1
a Aphrodite
b God of the underworld
c On Mount Olympus
d Hermes
e Sun, light, music and truth
f Athene

Exercise 2
Any appropriate picture of the Underworld – dark and fiery!

Exercise 3
A variety of answers are suitable, such as:
Dearest Achillea,
I went to the theatre today, up on the hillside. It was shaped like a horseshoe, with seats in tiers (or rows). Although I was a long way back, I could still hear the actors, because the acoustics were very good. The actors wore masks. The tragedy masks were quite spooky!
With love
Ariadne

Exercise 4
a Acoustics – How well sound travels
b Amplify – Make louder
c Comedy – Funny play
d Tragedy – Sad play
e Actors – People who pretend to be someone else to tell a story
f Audience – People watching a play or event
g Horseshoe – Semicircle shape

Exercise 5
a olympic
b games
c religious
d festival
e boxing
f horseback
g pankration
h javelin

Exercise 6
a Javelin and Discus

b 200 and 400 metres. There was also a long-distance race and a race where runners wore armour.

c Pankration was a mixture of wrestling and boxing. There were two kinds: one was to knock the opponent to the floor, the other was to knock the opponent out.

Page 21

i	n	d	u	s	e	s	b	v	w	c	h
t	t	n	o	i	s	r	u	c	x	e	b
o	o	u	n	t	r	l	s	s	d	a	a
m	c	u	l	t	u	r	a	l	x	r	n
b	e	x	c	a	v	a	t	e	d	t	c
s	e	n	a	l	w	m	z	k	w	s	i
c	b	m	w	e	c	t	k	i	p	c	e
c	i	v	i	l	i	s	a	t	i	o	n
h	e	a	d	a	p	p	a	r	a	h	t

Page 23
1 4th
2 3000
3 2200
4 370
5 80,000
6 1500
7 280,000

Page 25
Across
4 Indus
6 Harappa
8 excavation
9 pottery
10 remains

Down
1 Multan
2 Mohenjo-Daro
3 seal
5 discovery
7 Pakistan

Pages 26–27 Revision exercises
Exercise 1
a Pakistan and western India
b Harappan
c Most of it has not been excavated
d They need to work out the meaning of the written language

Exercise 2
a Of great age, very old
b A society which has developed rules and routines
c Grew – very successfully
d A trip or journey
e Collection of hidden treasure
f The culture of a place would include its books, music, plays – but also how the people thought

Exercise 3
a Indus valley
b 1500
c The earliest pyramids were being built
d Stonehenge was being built
e Ur
f 80,000

Exercise 4
a coastal
b prosperous
c millennium
d settlements
e civilisation
f pyramids

Exercise 5
a T b F c T d F e T f F

Exercise 6
a Remains
b Buddhist
c Excavations
d Seals
e Pottery
f Fragments
g Archaeologist

Page 29
1 granaries
2 community
3 emperor
4 Harappa
5 museum
6 Indus
7 drainage
8 houses
9 palace
10 washing

Page 31

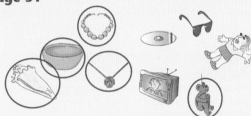

The objects not circled could not have been found because they are modern and are made from materials, such as plastic, which was not available at the time.

Page 33

b	i	t	u	m	e	n	b	v	w	c	h
a	t	e	e	n	p	i	h	s	r	o	w
t	o	u	n	t	r	l	s	s	d	a	d
h	d	u	n	o	i	g	i	l	e	r	x
b	e	n	a	c	u	a	t	e	d	t	v
s	e	n	c	l	o	i	s	t	e	r	a
c	h	a	n	g	i	n	g	i	s	c	a
p	u	r	i	f	i	c	a	t	i	o	n
h	e	f	o	o	r	p	r	e	t	a	w

Pages 34–35 Revision exercises

Exercise 1
a Burnt brick and stone
b The eastern part of the city
c The Lower Town
d No
e Two

Exercise 2
Many answers are correct
a The houses were made from burnt brick and stone. They were on two levels
b The bathrooms had toilets and washing platforms
c The water system included drainage systems, sewers, wells and water storage systems
d The granaries were large storehouses for the whole community

Exercise 3
a ✗ b ✔ c ✔ d ✔ e ✗ f ✔
g ✔ h ✗

Exercise 4
a purification   d deep
b worship   e ancient
c changing

Exercise 5
a It was made waterproof by soft bitumen being put on the bottom and sides of the pool
b Archaeologists think it may have been a meeting place or a place of worship

Exercise 6
An appropriate drawing including the main bath, some smaller baths, a cloister and changing rooms on three sides

Page 37

igloo, nest, dog, umbrella, shell / vase, ant, lemon, lemon, egg, yacht / cat, igloo, vase, igloo, lemon, igloo, shell, ant, tree, igloo, orange, nest

Page 39

Many answers are correct, including:

1 The excitement of discovering things
2 Imagining life from certain times in the past
3 Research
4 Going to museums
5 Working outside

Page 41

1 curator	6 history
2 museum	7 artefacts
3 exhibit	8 jigsaw
4 conserving	9 cleaned
5 reconstructed	10 restored

Pages 42–43 Revision exercises

Exercise 1
a Basalt   d Writing
b Hieroglyphics   e Scholar
c Rosetta Stone

Exercise 2
a A large piece of black rock with writing carved on it
b It showed Greek words and the corresponding hieroglyphs, and so allowed people to decipher the hieroglyphics
c Iratham Mahadevan and Dr Ahmad Hassan Dani
d Because it could tell historians a lot about life in the Indus valley civilisation

Exercise 3
Reading is fun

Exercise 4
a A historian finds out about life in the past. He or she asks a variety of questions such as who, what, where, and how. They have to do lots of research and be able to piece different clues and information together to find answers
b An archaeologist excavates sites and remains and finds the artefacts that end up in museums

Exercise 5
a Someone who works in and looks after a museum and its contents
b Make things last for a long time
c An object put on display
d A place where historical objects are stored, studied and displayed
e An old object, like those found on digs
f When someone's views affect choices and decisions they make
g The breakdown of something; when its condition gets worse

Exercise 6
Many answers can be correct. One example is:

Do you like history? Are you a good teacher?

Could you clean, restore and group artefacts from different periods of time?

If you can do all this and can make history exciting, then you could be a curator at a museum!